The micro theology series scratches an important itch: accessible books addressing crucial topics. And Jonathan Foster is the ideal author for this series. What a fantastic way to explore what matters most!

—Thomas Jay Oord, author of *Open and Relational Theology* and other books

I used to believe that God sacrificed himself to himself to save humanity from himself. But what if instead God was *at one* with Jesus dying on the cross and what if God is *at one* with us when we suffer? Jonathan Foster's "at-one-ment" is exactly just that!

—Mason Mennenga, YouTuber and podcast host of *A People's Theology*

What Jonathan gives us with this writing is a way to begin to disentangle violence from our religion and in the day and age we live in there may be nothing more important.

—Dana Hicks, author of *Quest for Thin Places: How to Find Spirituality after Deconstruction*

Jonathan Foster masterfully distills profound mysteries of the divine into accessible, soul-shaping wisdom for our liminal age. His writing, like a well in the desert, offers grounded nourishment to those dwelling in spiritual thresholds, revealing grace not as abstract theory but as embodied belonging. This is essential micro-theology for anyone hungry to encounter the sacred in the tension of transformation.

—Thomas Rundel, host of the *Liminal Living Podcast*

At-One-Ment

An Open and Relational
Take on Atonement

Jonathan J. Foster

Copyright © 2025 by Jonathan J. Foster

All rights reserved. This book or any portion thereof may not be reproduced or used in any manner whatsoever without the express written permission of the publisher except for the use of brief quotations in a book review or scholarly journal.

NO AI TRAINING: Without in any way limiting the author [and publisher's] exclusive rights under copyright, any use of this publication to "train" generative artificial intelligence (AI) technologies to generate text is expressly prohibited. The author reserves all rights to license uses of this work for generative AI training and development of machine learning language models.

Paperback: 978-1-968136-27-7
Ebook: 978-1-968136-06-2
Audio: 978-1-968136-07-9

Printed in the United States of America

Library of Congress Cataloguing-in-Publication Data
At-One-Ment: An Open and Relational Take on Atonement /
Jonathan J. Foster

For my sisters
lifelong friends
and the best of listeners

Table of Contents

Micro Theology Series Introduction 1
- Love is the Lens 3
- A Working Definition of Love 4
- I Believe in You 6

My Context 11
- Open and Relational Theology 11
- Mimetic Theory 12
- My Lived Experience with Three Inciting Incidents 13
- Now You Know 19

At-One-Ment: An Open and Relational Take on Atonement 21
- The Importance of the Concept 22

- A Few Things I Need to Say Before the Things I Need to Say. 23
- Common Atonement Ideas Around Which Western Christianity Revolves 25
  - 1. Ransom Theory 25
  - 2. Satisfaction Theory 26
  - 3. Moral Influence Theory 27
  - 4. Penal Substitutionary Atonement Theory 27
  - 5. Mimetic/Scapegoat 30
  - 6. Narrative Christus Victor (KRIS-tus VIK-tor). 32
  - 7. Liberation/Feminist Theology. 35
- My Atonement Theory 36

Some Comments from the Original Essay on Substack/Patreon. 43

A Few Books and Online Resources. 57

About the Author 59

Some Other Books in the Micro Theology Series 61

AI Disclosure 63

Micro Theology Series Introduction

Book 1: At-One-Ment

There's an old story that my friend likes to share about a woman who wanted to translate and distribute the scriptures to her community. For several years she saved her money until she had enough to pay someone for the translation. Just then, a pandemic hit her community. With her neighbors suffering and even dying by the dozens, she decided to spend her money on medicine to care for the sick.

Eventually, the pandemic ended, but not before it exhausted her savings. For several more years, she worked diligently until she once again had enough to pay for the translation. But then a famine struck.

Friends and neighbors were on the verge of starvation, so she took the money and bought food to keep them alive.

When the famine ended, she was broke. So, she started over. As she grew older, she saved every penny. Finally, at the end of her life, she was able to get the scriptures translated and distributed to her people.

For the remainder of that community's existence, whenever that story was told, someone would point out that the woman had translated the scriptures three times throughout her life . . . and the first two were the most powerful.

I love that story, and whatever I have to say about theology or one's approach to the bible can't be said better than what it communicates. It's probably apocryphal, but whenever I hear it, I recognize truth. The depth of truth is more than just a set of propositions lined out and bullet-pointed. The depth of truth is a relational movement motivated by love. Whatever spirit you sense from that woman—whatever matrix of reasoning she used when faced with those difficult choices—that's the point. Honestly, that's it. To add more words, micro-expression or not, is to risk getting off track. So, you should probably be careful with what follows.

Love is the Lens

The micro theology series is "micro" in word count only—these topics span a wide breadth of theological inquiry, presented in accessible, Substack/Patreon-sized reflections. My goal is to help you, the reader, engage theology through a lens marked less by closed minded dogmatism and more by open-ended reasoning. Which is to say, I hope to help you fashion a lens of love. This is not only permissible; it's what the bible with its undeniable interest in powerless nations, scorned victims, and scapegoated saviors, encourages us to do.

Note: this isn't a lens-free approach. Such an approach doesn't exist, for none of us comes to a text outside of a *context*. Context is informed by a variety of imitative, symbolic, and conceptual factors, all of which necessarily present themselves differently in different periods, cultures, traditions, languages, and families. Which means that when it comes to reading scripture, even if we knew the exact word or phrase that any one of the biblical writers used, there is little chance that strict, definitive meanings from *their* day could be imported into exact understandings of *our* day. Insisting otherwise would be like using bronze-age tools to work out digital-age problems.

Words are fluid. They must be, for their definitions are filtered through the relationship of language and culture, neither of which are static. However, the capital-W Word, filtered through truth and spirit, is also fluid. Sometimes, the capital-W Word gets lost in the lowercase-w words, but if we're aware, discerning, vulnerable, and courageous, we might gain the wisdom to see the capital-W Word transcending and including the lowercase-w words.

In case I'm being too poetic, let me be clear: the hope of scripture (lowercase-w words) is the way all of this plays out within the life of Jesus, the Christ (the capital-W Word). Embodied love is the fulfillment of our text. The strength of what the bible offers is not definitive rigidity around rules; the strength is the way words and stories get inside, influence, and then work their way out into healthy, interrelated lives. I name this love, and I'm in agreement with the Apostle Paul who once wrote to his Galatian friends and said, "The only thing that matters is faith expressing itself in love."

A Working Definition of Love

I don't have the final word, but my working definition of love is that it is an uncontrolling, nonbinary, nonviolent, non-scapegoating energy entangled with

God and everyone that's meant for the non-complete flourishing of everything.

- Uncontrolling because if something controls, I find it difficult to call it love.

- Nonbinary because love isn't interested in pitting one thing against another.

- Nonviolent because violence probably isn't love.

- Non-scapegoating because I've come to believe that much religion is built upon a mechanism of blame. I'd like to distance myself from the practice.

- Energy because love isn't exactly a person or a thing.

- Entangled because where God ends, and creation begins is impossible to determine.

- The flourishing of everything because love is so creative that it can lift one thing up without tearing another thing down.

- Non-complete flourishing because I don't think the point of love is to provide wholeness to the degree that you no longer have desire. Desire doesn't work that way. Wanting is fueled by the not-having. It's the lack that produces the energy. So, flourishing isn't necessarily completeness or filling the lack with anything (including with God) so that you are whole. No, the depth of flourishing allows lack to be with you on the journey of love.

I Believe in You

So, this is an approach that encourages you, the reader, the human being, the person privileged to be the steward of this lived experience to choose a lens of love. (An uncontrolling, nonbinary, nonviolent, non-scapegoating energy entangled with God and everyone that's meant for the non-complete flourishing of everything.)

"Wait," I hear you asking, "can I do that?"

Yes! Yes, you can. Love *wants* you to think through these things for yourself. Notice the words of Jesus in Luke 8:18: "consider carefully how you listen."

Look, you already have a context. But this doesn't mean you can't *influence* your context. I know such an idea might cause you anxiety, particularly if you're coming from a religious system that's told you you're incapable of determining your own ideas; that's conditioned you from day one to believe that your heart is "deceitful above all things." But consider that this kind of message has come to you within a certain environment (again, context). Meanwhile, you are free to form your own opinions.

I want to tell you the same thing I told three young women recently at a coffee shop who were probably around the age of my daughter. I couldn't help but notice, as they sat next to me praying, discussing, and drinking coffee, that next to their bibles was a book by a well-known preacher, someone who has made a living off telling young women, just like them, that they cannot lead, teach, or preach, at least, not when men are present.

I cringed, turned the music in my headphones up, and did my best not to think about their limited context. My distraction strategy didn't work. I kept thinking about these young women, their future, *everyone's* future. About an hour later, on my way out, I did my best to respectfully offer my opinion: "Despite what the author of the book you're reading thinks," I said, taking the time to look each of them in the eye, "I believe in you."

And that's what I want to say to you. You are capable and strong. You're empowered and free. You have permission to co-partner with the divine to figure out how to grow and make your best judgment about everything, especially the way scripture will inform your theology. You can't control the lens, but you can *shape* the lens, and what better way to shape than with love? So, yes, bring love into the reading of the text. Watch how it influences your understanding.

- Love with you in Joshua 6, as God commands Joshua to kill every man, woman, child, cow, sheep, and donkey. How do you think love wants you to interpret such a command?

- Love with you in John 8, when the religious leaders, preaching holiness, rules, and consequences, drag the woman caught in adultery to Jesus. What is love asking you when Jesus says, "Let him without sin throw the first stone?"

- And love with you throughout the Book of Revelation, as you read about a quasi-religious imperialistic government marking people in a particular way. Is love saying anything about the way quasi-christian, neo-imperialism has marked you?

Years of reading and studying, thinking and praying, talking with lay people and scholars, writing books and getting degrees have led me to believe the following: One can utilize the bible to get to messages about love, or one can utilize love to get to messages in the bible. I choose the latter.

Whoever has an ear to hear, let them hear.

My Context

Speaking of contexts, mine has been marked by two distinct but overlapping paradigms in the midst of my lived experience. Each of these has played and continues to play a significant role in the shaping and influencing of my story.

Open and Relational Theology

Open and relational theology, a phrase coined by Thomas Jay Oord, rallies around two ideas:

First, that God experiences time moment by moment, the result of which is an undetermined future (i.e., open). The future has not yet happened, so it is, unknowable. An open view rejects the notion of a

God with exhaustive divine foreknowledge of all future events. This doesn't mean that God isn't aware of patterns or have good ideas of how things are going to play out, but fixed outcomes make little sense if God is love.

Second, that God is deeply interconnected with creation (i.e., relational). The fundamental building block of all creation, from the micro to the macro, is not independent and substance-based; rather, it is interdependent and relationship-based. This is true of the cosmos and, again, of God. Therefore, a relational view rejects the notion of a God that's separate, unable to experience, and impervious to change. Whatever God is, S(H)e is dynamic, interactive, experiential, and intimately related to all creation. Separateness makes little sense if God is love.

Mimetic Theory

René Girard's (zhee-RAHRD) mimetic theory resists neat summarization, but since it would make little sense for me to talk about my context, without mentioning the theory, I'll offer the briefest of explanations:

Mimetic theory explores how our desires are shaped through relationship and imitation of others, how those desires can become rivalrous and generate conflict, and how this process drives us toward scapegoating as a remedy. Unfortunately, scapegoating works, in fact, it works so well that we've relied on it repeatedly over the millennia, and it's in this repetition that Girard sees religion being born. As challenging and pessimistic as this all is, for the christian, there may be hope, for there is a way to understand that what Jesus was doing was to become a scapegoat to reveal our addiction to scapegoating religion and to subvert the whole mechanism from the inside out. And I suspect that *is* what has happened.

You can learn about both open and relational theology and mimetic theory in one book, by reading *Theology of Consent: Mimetic Theory in an Open and Relational Universe*.

My Lived Experience with Three Inciting Incidents

As important as both those ideas have been, it's possible that neither of them would have been that interesting to me if my life had gone in a different direction. But my lived experience has shaped me profoundly, particularly those events that I sometimes refer to as "inciting incidents."

An inciting incident is a literary phrase—a way to characterize how tension provides "traction" in a story, propelling it forward toward resolution. Here are three inciting incidents that have shaped and continue to shape my story:

First, I kept meeting people who were not only different from me; they were different from what the church system normally produced. Of course, any system that wishes to exist must produce and reproduce people who fit well within their system. This isn't all that surprising or concerning. What's concerning is how the church system tends to do this in the name of God.

Therefore, if a church system isn't careful, or refuses to listen to outside voices, or lacks awareness of the powerless, it will send the message that Godly people tend to vote the same, express themselves sexually in similar ways, occupy the same social-economic standing, and generally believe all the same kinds of things.

But I kept meeting real, live human beings that didn't fit the mold. Even more, I discovered that many of these outside-the-mold people were genuine, intelligent, and really thoughtful. Each interaction made it increasingly clear that what we held in common was greater than what we didn't. People would leave my office, and in so many words, I would think, "Oh, gosh, I think that person who doesn't fit my system is more put together than most of the people I know who *do* fit the system!"

Meanwhile, irrespective of differences, what I intuited time and time again was that unconditional and uncontrolling love was for these people just as much as it was for me.

A second category of inciting incident had to do with the inconsistencies I kept encountering within the sacred text. After a while, I could no longer live in denial about a handful of inconsistencies:

- Sometimes, these issues were something like a science problem. (Wait, archeologists haven't found evidence to support all the details of Israel's journey into the Promised Land? Wait, evolution doesn't rule out the possibility of love and, therefore, the possibility of the divine? God and evolution can co-exist?)

- Sometimes, the issues were anachronistic in that they had to do with how events were presented one way, only to be presented another way in a later passage. (Wait, so in Chronicles, it's Satan that tempts David, but when the same story is told in Samuel, it's Yahweh? Hold on, in Mark's account of the resurrection, it was a young man in white appearing to three women, but in Matthew's account, it was an angel appearing to only one woman?)

- Some of my issues had to do with the difficulty of translation itself. I began recognizing that even within my lifetime, the meaning of certain words had changed or were changing. As I considered translating texts over 2,500 years, in some cases from languages that were no longer even used, and I considered changing customs, traditions, and cultural shifts, I knew it was no longer reasonable to expect any modern-day bible to be 100% error-free. (Time out, the Greek word *metanoia* means change your way of thinking rather than repent? And the Hebrew name *El Shaddai* means "I am the breasted God" and not The Almighty?)

- And finally, some of my problems had to do with the reality of incompatible messaging. (Let me get this straight, in the very same passage that people were told to stone gay people, they were also told to love their neighbor. How does that work? What do you do if your

> neighbor is gay? How do you stay biblical and love your neighbor but stay biblical and stone your neighbor?)

Some inconsistencies were more acute than others, but the point is, all of these and many others served to catalyze questions.

The well-intentioned bible-loving christian often respond to these questions in the only way they know how, which is to flatly quote 2Timothy 3:16 and assert that "ALL scripture is inspired." But, even if we ignored the circular logic employed by using the text to say that the text is inspired, you should still be aware that at the time Timothy was reading that line, the only existing scriptures were the first five books of the Old Testament and writing from the prophets.

The entirety of what the Protestant-West now calls the bible, wasn't ratified for *another 300+ years.* During that time, the fight over which books would and would not be thought of as "inspired" was intense, full of disagreement, banishments, and excommunications. And since that time? Good grief, look at history. Debates about how to think of scripture have launched a thousand book burnings, excommunications, skirmishes, and wars.

Whatever else is going on with "inspired scripture," the text itself doesn't need to be thought of as infallible, inerrant, or without error. Such thinking only opens the door to the previously mentioned insanity.

There are healthier moves to make with the concept of "inspired." Here are three:

1. It's inspired to help the reader see the stupidity of trying to establish power by way of words, *particularly when the words talk so much about love.*

2. It's inspired to help the reader see that using certain passages about grace to decode other passages about violence is an intelligent move.

3. What the bible is inspired to do is help the reader be introduced to an *inspired messiah.*

My third category of inciting incident can be summed up with one word: loss. There are too many to list here, and I write about grief more in my book *indigo: the color of grief,* but sicknesses, fires, the loss of denominational estimation (in official and unofficial ways), tragedies, car wrecks, and the deaths of multiple family members—sometimes under violent and absurd situations—all impacted the way I engaged with theology and scripture. Loss changed me in many ways, not least in that it left me feeling powerless.

Being out of power not only destabilized the way I related to God and the way I read scripture, it also altered the way I related to others who had experience with loss. I don't mean to suggest that a straight, white, American, relatively affluent and educated, christian male—someone who obviously checks all the power boxes—can completely relate to the Native American, the trafficked, the queer, the families forever changed by slavery, the women, the divorced, the migrant, the abused, or any number of other individuals and people groups who have suffered.

I'm uninterested in appropriating their pain; however, if my loss has done anything for me, it's helped me see how powerlessness, in general, can inform one's theology in powerful ways.

Now You Know

So, now you know a bit about what I've been through. It's important, particularly as I'm trying to help you begin to work through theological issues, that I'm honest about what I've been through and how it motivated me in my theological studies. All of this (and more) has contributed to why I've shaped the lens through which I interpret life, as best I can, into a lens of love.

I've tried other approaches, but none have provided much life, at least not for long. Take your pick: a doubling down on holiness living, deference to denomination, confession of creeds, bible memorization, church attendance, giving large percentages of my income away, going on missions trips, not to mention rooting out all immorality by going through long seasons of "taking every thought captive." (Ha, that last one can sure take some time.) None of that has really helped me all that much, and much of it left me feeling a bit helpless. The thing that *has* brought hope, really, genuinely, is love.

If you're uninterested in love, fair enough. If that's the case, then the micro-theology series, influenced as it is by open and relational thinking, probably isn't for you. However, if you're sensing an invitation to cultivate a new approach—one that's creative, open-ended, and inclusive, which both requires *and* increases intellectual honesty, then maybe this will be the start of something new for you.

I hope so.

At-One-Ment: An Open and Relational Take on Atonement

Atonement, the suffering of Jesus on the cross, is a process, an event, a happening—like a sunset or sunrise. It has two time zones. It happened more than two millennia ago, and it is happening still today. Both are important. The event, freed from ideas of penal substitution, is powerful, tragic, and quietly beautiful. It reveals divine suffering and the power of forgiveness; and it opens up a historic possibility tremendously important today: a renewal of love amid tragedy. This event depends on other events for its meaning. It cannot stand alone as the single point of Christianity. But Christianity without the cross is not Christianity at all. It hides from suffering in the interests of prosperity or pleasure. A more holistic

Christianity includes the whole of life, the thorns and the roses, the sins and the gifts. the need for love and the need for forgiveness.

—Jay McDaniel

The Importance of the Concept

For as little as I use the word "atonement," I sure interact with it a lot. I think this is true for at least three reasons:

1. My conclusion that God didn't need the death of Jesus in order to forgive was a theological watershed moment for me. Like the Continental Divide that sends rainwater to different oceans, this realization redirected all my thoughts about God, life, and humanity into completely new theological waters.

2. There is no doubt in my mind that our prevailing atonement ideas influence and shape our prevailing cultural issues—racism, climate change, or nationalism. Therefore, the topic is relevant.

3. Whenever I broach this subject—essay, book, text, email, or Instagram post someone

somewhere messages me with questions and comments. It's true; sometimes, the questions and comments begin with "How dare you?" "Shame on you," and "You are wrong on this one," but often, the comments and questions begin with "Wow, I never knew this," "Thank you, this changes a lot," and "If this is true, then a lot of the religious stuff I do is messed up."

To the former group: "Okay. God bless. I hope the best for you." And to the latter: "Yes and amen."

A Few Things I Need to Say Before the Things I Need to Say

My rundown here will be too brief for those initiated into all-things atonement. My apologies, but my goal is to interact with readers who have not taken time to dive deeply into this topic.

If you're looking for a bunch of verses that you can spend all day flipping back and forth to in your leather-bound Thompson Chain Reference Bible, this will leave you disappointed. I might add some in a follow-up writing, but as of this moment, I'm fatigued with all the proof-texting that goes on with this discussion, and my lived experience is this if a person is unwilling to see how much their context, their own religious condition, and their own biases play into the way they read Scripture, *it doesn't matter how many bible verses I add.*

Each of these following ideas has some biblical merit, and as I often say ... there is a way to read the bible (or any text for that matter) that would lead you to think that controlling, sacrificial violence is a necessary component of love's story, *I just don't think it's the healthiest way to read the bible (or any text for that matter).*

If we don't give our best thinking to reading things in a healthy way, then eventually, we will all follow the propagandists (and the power-hungr*iest* and the scapegoat-*ists*, too) to a violent end.

I have defined health in other writing, but in a nutshell, I'm thinking of something that never stops attempting to access love, patience, creativity, grace, dialogue, consent, non-violence, and the empowerment of those who've been marginalized all in a non-coercive and uncontrolling way. Yes, that sounds like a measure of health to me.

And finally, look, I know that I'm eager to define and redefine the events of Jesus' life, especially those that took place during what we sometimes refer to as the passion story, in light of uncontrolling love. I consider a commitment to uncontrolling love to be of utmost importance here. Yet, I confess that I often write (and live) with an impatience that undermines my commitment.

Common Atonement Ideas Around Which Western Christianity Revolves

1 - Ransom Theory: As the name implies, the idea here is that Jesus gave his life as an exchange or payment. The question became, to whom is the ransom paid? Some claim that the payee was Satan, but this is problematic. I don't know about you, but I'm not entirely comfortable with God needing to be in bondage to Satan. (Not to mention that the way the colloquial way a name like "Satan" is tossed about is probably not the same idea that the Hebrew writers had when they used the name, which is for a whole other book, but worth mentioning here.)

Another take is to say that Jesus paid or exchanged something to God, and essentially, this *is* the Western evangelical position. But I find picturing God as a father making demands from his Son to get his other children off the hook even more troubling than a satanic force making such demands.

It's difficult, in our culture, to distance the word ransom from anything outside of something we see as transactional, and therefore, I never use the word. Still, if I had to, I'd use it in a way that recognizes that when Jesus gave his life, he did so *to free us from the prison of our own existential fear, the kind of fear that's driven us to create religions of scapegoating violence.*

2 - Satisfaction Theory: This emerged from a theologian named Anselm during medieval feudalism, a time when honoring land barons, lords, and kings played a vital role in a functioning economic system.

Anselm's idea was that our sin has dishonored God, and something God cannot ignore. But given that sacrifices made by imperfect humans always fell short of a perfect and holy God, how would God make sure his honor is restored? To complicate matters, according to proponents of this theory, God himself was the only one who can truly fix the problem. No one else contained God's power, so obviously, it was God who had to fix God. So, he became human and, with his death, restored his own sense of justice, and yes, all of this brought him infinite "satisfaction."

(I often think of David Bentley Hart's line here, "Like a bank issuing itself credit to pay off a debt it owes itself, using a currency it has minted for the occasion and certified in its value wholly on the basis of the very credit it is issuing to itself.")

The satisfaction theory, like the ransom theory (and, as we'll see, similar to the penal substitutionary theory), is not something I'd categorize as good news. Not only does it have God satisfied because God allowed his only son to be killed in an effort to fix God's problem, it emphasizes our separation from the divine, it elevates the death of Jesus over the ethics of Jesus, and the entire idea is completely dependent upon sacrificial violence.

3 - Moral Influence: In response to the satisfaction theory, a French theologian, Peter Abelard, created the moral influence theory. Abelard understood that Jesus showed up, lived, taught, healed, forgave, and ultimately died to influence humanity toward moral improvement. Instead of satisfying God's justice or honor, Jesus' death was designed to impress the world with a sense of God's love. While I don't use the moral influence phrase much, I align with any thinking that understands God's action harmonizing with love and acceptance vs. transactional violent sacrifice.

4 - The Penal Substitutionary Atonement Theory (P-S-A). Okay, big breath . . . P-S-A is a mashup of ransom and satisfaction theories, so see all the aforementioned problems there. To complicate matters, courtesy of the last couple of hundred years of modernity, P-S-A usually comes freighted with some additional economic, judicial, and authoritarian baggage.

- The economic baggage, as I have heard it preached (more than once!), causes us to see Jesus as something like a benevolent, rich bystander who, upon learning of the overwhelming debt we've incurred against God, steps in, at the last minute and pays the incomprehensibly large sum to God, who in this illustration, can only be seen as the Great Miserly Banker in the Sky.

- The judicial baggage, again something I've heard or read countless times, causes us to see Jesus as a good lawyer who approaches God as The Great Judge in the Sky and argues for us. Apparently, in this scenario, the skill of Jesus convinces God, but only to a certain extent because, in the end, the lawyer himself must take our place. In other words, The Judge's conception of forgiveness is directly attached to sacrificial violence.

- The authoritarian baggage suggests that even though you and I know to ignore authoritarian hierarchy and call Child Protection Services when we learn about a parent abusing a child, in the case of God and his son, abuse is not only permitted; it's glorified.

To add to the problematic way all of this unfolds, there is precious little questioning going on within the P-S-A camp about the "extra" violence that accompanies the crucifixion. Questions such as, "What is the point of the scourging, beating, and torture in the Passion Story? How does such absurd violence serve God? How much torture was enough torture? What was the tipping point for God—the 40th whiplash, the third, no fourth stake into his body, the 87th jeer, the 25th slap to the face? All of this, PLUS his final breath?"

These questions are as necessary as they are nauseating, and they are *the tip of the proverbial iceberg lodged into the side of the P-S-A-Titanic*. Meanwhile, unfortunately, most evangelical Christians assume P-S-A to be **The Gospel**, rather than a sacrificially-driven interpretation popularized a couple of hundred years ago. It's had a *profound* impact on the development of the United Empire of America (i.e., manifest destiny, slavery, politics, etc . . .), but it is *not* the gospel.

There are some really wonderful people who subscribe to P-S-A. I know this to be true. I won't get into all the reasons why or *how* this could be, as I try to do that in other places; nevertheless, I happen to think that a God of love dependent upon sacrificial violence is the worst thinking ever invented and is a virus that's infected the operating system of Americanized-christianity.

5 - Mimetic / Scapegoat: Technically, what René Girard offers with his mimetic/scapegoating theory is not an atonement theory, although many have found it to be a torch to light their way out of the darkness cast by P-S-A.

The mimetic/scapegoating theory reveals people's deep-seated need to "offload" their psycho-spiritual problems onto the back of the other, which causes them to identify the other as the problem. All of which leads them to rid themselves of said problem. The peace that can sweep over a community after such scapegoating (i.e., shunning, kicking out, excommunicating, lynching, victimizing, crucifying, etc.) fools them into believing that the whole thing has been divinely inspired.

The peace doesn't last, of course, and when antagonism builds back up, the community sequences the process all over again at the expense of a new victim. It's in this re-sequencing that the process becomes sacralized and eventually materializes into religion. Therefore, for Girard, violence doesn't stem from our religion as much as *religion stems from our violence.*

It's impossible to read the Passion Story as one did before, once one becomes aware of this insight. Jesus didn't use mimetic theory language, of course, but, in a sense, he diagnosed the victimizing system and became the antidote. He did this by inserting himself into the system as an innocent human. He became a scapegoat to END all scapegoating, which was never something God needed, but something *we* needed. What he demonstrated was how much the system owed its existence to our anxiety, shame, violence, and fear rather than anything we could have ascribed to God.

The resurrection continued the revelation because not only did Jesus reappear, but he reappeared without inspiring mimetic violence. Incredibly, instead of pursuing vengeance, he went even further down the path he had already initiated—a path of non-violent forgiveness, mercy, grace, empowerment, consent, and estimation of *all* people, particularly the marginalized. I write more about this in Theology of Consent: Mimetic Theory in an Open and Relational Universe.

6 - Narrative Christus Victor: The church, before Constantine and state-assimilated Christianity, in those first 300 years of its existence, probably viewed this entire discussion quite differently than it does now. It'd be impossible to nuance this as much as it deserves in one micro-book, so I'm pulling this theory together under Denny J. Weaver's heading: Narrative Christus Victor.

I greatly appreciate the lengths Weaver and others have gone in not reducing salvation down to the last bloody, violent, shuddering breath of Jesus. For Narrative Christus Victor, it's important to embrace the *entire narrative* of Jesus. What's the narrative? Well, it's too much to recite here, but it includes key components such as . . .

- Launching his public ministry by announcing good news to the poor,

- Backing up that announcement by going out of his way for the orphan, widow, foreigner, woman, and diseased (i.e., those without representation within the religious-patriarchal system of his day),

- Breaking ceremonial laws, customs, and taboos,

- Standing up to the religious elite,

- Refusing to use violence,

- And offering grace and forgiveness to all people.

This last point is significant, particularly as we consider that Jesus offered forgiveness *before* his violent death. (A serious meditation on just this one idea would destabilize the entirety of P-S-A.)

There's too much to include here (ha, read the Gospels, man), but it's safe to say that Jesus's disposition, attitude, and actions generated some pushback from the religious, political, and economic sectors. What the opposition lacked in integrity, they made up for in good old-fashion industrial cowardice as they figured out how to . . .

- Trap Jesus under the cover of darkness,

- Throw together a kangaroo court,

- Fabricate some accusations,

- Secure an unjust sentence,

- And incite a mob all within a few hours.

They worked so quickly that they were able to murder him in time to get his body off the cross before sunrise of the next day, their Sabbath, lest they be found guilty of doing any work on their holy day. Because you want to be lawful when you murder someone.

I pause to point out that Narrative Christus Victor includes *all* of these details and more in the story of atonement. Again, their point is to distance themselves from the simplistic reductionistic view that Jesus was born to die. What's included in these details, quite obviously, is a savior who eschews violence at every turn.

Meanwhile, in my understanding, Narrative Christus Victor would align well with the Eastern church in seeing the death of Jesus like the death of a seed that falls into the ground, then breaks open and grows from the inside out. The Eastern Church has a great tradition of telling fantastic Easter stories about how the event might have occurred deep within and behind the gates of Hades/Sheol/afterlife. However it took place, the idea was that God went into the very source of the enemy's strength and won a decisive victory from the inside out, announcing the good news that *we are no longer in need of being held captive to our existential fear of death.*

Finally, as if any of this is final, the story of Jesus includes some important post-resurrection elements. It cannot be overstated: when Jesus returned from the dead, he wasn't in military fatigues making his way back into the streets of Jerusalem with the intent of initiating a coup! No, not at all. Just the opposite. When he returned, he was mistaken for a gardener! Ha, I love how the Hebrew story starts in a garden and then has its most significant plot twist in a garden.

7 - I'm going to combine Liberation and Feminist theology for the last entry, for both groups are exceptional at reading the story aware of the systemic injustice humans are known to perpetuate.

These groups will always reserve suspicion, and rightly so, for anyone who claims marginalized people need to sacrifice anything, let alone their life, to gain someone's liberation. It's quite understandable why they think this way . . . *it's because their group is always the first to be called upon when someone needs to be sacrificed.*

Liberation and Feminist thinkers are right to point out that if the story promotes an innocent man submitting to an unjust murder, something initiated by his authoritarian father no less, then it opens the door for the powerful to demand that the powerless remain in abusive situations.

Likewise, it opens the door to tell the powerless, in general, to stay in abusive sacrificial systems in the hope that being submissive just might change the hearts and minds of those in power. Check that last sentence, for it does more than "open the door," the reality is that *this has already happened* (i.e., abusive christian husbands, abusive white christian slaveholders, etc . . .)

Good Lord, nothing should make us angrier than when power-hungry christians hold onto abusive theology for their own gain. Ultimately, what these theological groups teach me, and this is a quote, more or less, from my friend Catherine Keller, is **"to worry less about what any of this says about atonement and worry more about the kind of power structures certain atonement theories create."** Amen.

My Atonement Theory

Ha! One should never write the sentence: "My atonement theory." And yet, palm to face, I just did. I do so hesitantly because I'm really not that interested in getting boxed into any one way of framing this whole thing. I'm looking to get out of boxes, not in them.

At-One-Ment

Then again, though all boxes are probably wrong, *some are less wrong than others.*

I'm committed to love. Not a kitschy, hallmark, pop-song kind of love. No, I'm committed to something deeper: an uncontrolling, non-violent, non-scapegoating, nonbinary energy in relationship with God and creation, that's actively seeking the non-complete flourishing of everyone and everything kind of love.

I'm committed to this because of its philosophical and biblical depth. And because it seems that Jesus was committed to this kind of love, too. It is no small thing for me to read about an itinerate, impoverished, powerless, brown-skinned man embodying these concepts that, frankly, I've spent years of my life vetting. *Do you know what I mean?* Like, when you discover concepts, language, truth, and story that light up all your psycho-spiritual and neurological pathways and then find someone who lived it out in real, flesh and blood ways? Yeah, that's exciting. All this kind of thinking informs the lens through which I view a word like atonement.

When I use the word, or read it, I think ***at-one-ment.*** I think that the work of love that's embodied in Jesus is an active, ongoing work of communicating to the world, over and over, that the divine is *at one* with us. That we are all, in essence, *at one* with each other. That this whole thing is *one*, very large movement, albeit with countless smaller movements.

What takes place at the cross is a non-linear prism of truth:

- The truth that God is *at one* with our suffering.

- The truth that love (for I don't know how else to think of God other than love) contains something deep and wounded within itself. I can't explain that here, but I invite you to read my book "indigo: the color of grief" or listen to an episode called "Cheese in the Darkness" from the "jonathan_foster podcast"—that's with an underscore between the names

- The truth that love is vulnerable and cannot single-handedly control.

- The truth that violence and entropy (even violent entropy), is reality.

- The truth that Jesus is innocent and *at one* with all victims everywhere.

- The truth that God is/was *at one* with Jesus. (In other words, he wasn't wringing his hands, back turned, hoping a sacrifice would show up that would be big enough to convince him to turn and face his son.)

- The truth that the death of Jesus isn't a requirement of love; it is a *revelation* of love.

- The truth that mercy is greater than sacrifice.

- The truth that humanity's modern-ancient story (by modern-ancient, I mean the move from a hunter-gatherer to an agrarian society, which is, roughly speaking, the move we're still in) has been corrupted by an unholy trinity of existential insecurity, mimetic and violent desire, and idolatrous hope in authoritarian power.

- The truth that the hope of the world lies in our willingness to admit our culpability in all the ways that the unholy trinity plays out. Therefore, we were all *at one* with the Roman political system, the religious elite, and the entire mob in the murder of Jesus.

- The truth that the cross isn't where everything is fixed; it's where everything is held together. Okay, maybe this is more a faith than truth thing, either way, it's certainly more a therapeutic than judicial thing, which sets me up to quote Gregory of Nazianzus: "That which is not assumed cannot be healed." (assumed = *at one* with.)

- The truth that the hope of the world lies in our willingness to be *at one* with the way Jesus returned from his murder, which was marked by peace, patience, hope, and forgiveness.

- The truth that love is *at one* with everything in such a deep way that even the worst things can turn out to be the best things. Look, if deicide (the murder of God) turning into resurrection and life isn't the best coming out of the worst, I don't know what is.

These truths are part faith, part revelation, part fact, and part mythic for when I speak of truth here, I'm not just talking about honesty, as in someone is telling the truth, but even more, I'm talking about structural integrity, as in the way we might talk about a building or a bridge that has structural integrity.

And can a home or a bridge be factual and mythic? Yes, actually it can. A home can be both a solid factual house and a place where a family grows in love. A bridge can both be a factual apparatus and a metaphor connecting people from one part of their story to the next part of their story. I'm betting my life, *honestly, I really am,* that what played out in the story of Jesus, nowhere more so than those last few days of his life, was a truth that contains all of the above.

More than ideas to entertain, lessons to learn, or doctrine to indoctrinate, all of it amounts to an invitation . . . an invitation to change our mind (repent) about the way we keep thinking we're separate from the divine and each other . . . an invitation to be at one with everything . . . an invitation to see that being at one with everything could very well cost us everything we have . . . and an invitation to have faith in the paradoxical idea that **loss is the way to gain.**

Yeah, it's really just an invitation . . . that's my atonement theory.

Some Comments from the Original Essay on Substack/Patreon

Note: This includes some, but not all, of the comments. Also, I made minor alterations to a few words to try and help narrators for the audio version.

 Reader Comment 1

Hi Jonathan—I welcome your view on at-one-ment and the uncontrolling love of God. Thank you. A phrase that I often find applied to myself is "We can be right in that which we affirm and wrong in that which we deny". I think it would be fair to say that it would not be proof texting if I should say that the substitutionary work of the Cross is a major theme of Paul in both Romans and Galatians especially.

In my writings (and I am not very good at it) I am trying to explore the freedom that Christ brings through his death. I have read Paul Tournier's "Guilt and Grace" and have started reading Luther's Commentary on Galatians and recognize that guilt and shame are the primary inhibitors to human development. I take it that God can just forgive and that forgiveness is what issued from the Cross when Jesus cried "Forgive them . . ." and believe that this love is uncontrolling, non coercive and life transforming.

Also, however, I believe something *did* happen at the Cross whereby all legal requirements that we place upon a controlling Deity are removed and through Christ we stand complete in the unconditional love of God. The Law is not only the reason sin exists ("Without the law there would be no sin" Romans 7), but also through the law "comes the knowledge of sin",. Furthermore "The actual power of sin is in the law". Paul's psychology and reasoning are most liberating when he said through the death of Christ we with Him are DEAD to the law—Dead means dead—unresponsive and disconnected and free to live in the wide place of Love.

I have considered that the language Paul uses may just be appropriate to the Jewish sacrificial milieu of the time and used as a metaphor for the liberation experienced for the Christian . . . or it could be literal. Whatever, there is contained within Paul's writings concerning the believers' freedom from the law, couched in terms we may find inappropriate, what can only be explained as containing a "joy unspeakable and full of glory"!

To abandon that would be to rob people who, struggling with guilt and shame are desperately trying to impress others, their conscience, and their idea of God, of a freedom which is theirs with no strings attached.

> **jonathan_foster Response**
>
> Thank you for your comment. I clicked over and read your post. Your style of writing is nice. Keep it up.
>
> And I like the content of where you are going. (Not that it matters what I "like," just that I resonate with some or maybe much of what you are saying.) Isn't it interesting that when something of great truth happens, it can be viewed and talked about from a handful of different perspectives? This is what I was trying to say when

I mentioned, "What takes place at the cross is a non-linear prism of truth." As I was reading your work, it felt like interesting prismatic stuff was happening.

And yes, I agree, it would be fair to point out that substitutionary thinking cannot just be thrown out . . . and at the same time, as we leave it in, questions should be forming around the concept, namely, for most of Americanized-christianity, "Who was the substitution for . . . and for what purpose?" If God needed a substitute to pour his wrath upon as the typical P-S-A, Ransom, or Satisfaction theories propose, then, well, I've already said as much, but "No thank you."

However, if we were the ones who needed a substitute . . . something to subvert the scapegoating mechanism called religion that we created . . . someone who, because of their innocence, was able to slip past the carefully crafted systems of shame, guilt, and non-reflexive sacrifice, then I would say "Yes."

And in that vein, to borrow from Richard Rohr, "The death of Jesus didn't change God's mind about us, but changed our mind about God." All of this is in alignment with what I heard you saying about our problem of guilt and shame. From a René Girard point of view, guilt, and shame can be seen as the fuel that drives the scapegoating engine.

And yes, to your sentence that says, "I have considered that the language Paul uses may just be appropriate to the Jewish sacrificial milieu of the time," (and I would also add to the Roman sacrificial milieu.)

Have you read James Alison? I thought of him while I was reading your comment. Check out, among other things, "Undergoing God: Dispatches from a Scene of a Break-In." I suspect that what he's saying harmonizes with what you are saying and, at times, might give an even more interesting (prismatic) look to all of this.

I'm still considering your 3rd paragraph . . . about what did happen at the cross. You might be right. I'm unsure of how to process this at this moment.

Thanks again for your "prismatic thoughts."

All my best

Reader Comment 2

How does the resurrection of Jesus and of all fit within your model of atonement? Have your views on that changed at all?

> **jonathan_foster Response**
>
> Great question (and I've had others ask the same thing this week) . . . for me, again, I don't really think of it as a model of atonement. Ha, despite the fact that I just wrote 4,000 words about it, "atonement" isn't in my vernacular; however, at-one-ment is!
>
> Once I decided that at-one-ment was the reality, then the story of the resurrection did at least two things . . .
>
> 1-It allows me to read the thing in a truthful way that incorporates revelation, mythic, faith, in a factual kind of way. (As I wrote about in the end of the post). Is the idea of resurrection factual? Well, one response might, "Hey, look at the butterfly!" It's a different organism (although very much attached to the previous caterpillar organism), and a whole new way of interacting

in the world that could've only been dreamed about by the caterpillar (Ha, supposing that caterpillars dream). Another response might be, "Look at the entire season we call spring. Something new is happening, though yes, it's attached to winter." What's true with spring and with butterflies is probably true in a variety of other ways, too.

I imagine the Jesus resurrection could be the same. Did it factually happen? I don't know for sure. I hope so. The followers went to their death claiming it to be true. And it seems, the tomb *was* empty. All those things are good indicators, but either way, wow, what a great mythic/faith/revelation story to orient my life around.

2-It allows me to see the commitment of Jesus being at one with everything. He was so at one ... that when he re-appeared he didn't stoop to violence, vengeance, retaliation, but elevated himself (and us) to grace, forgiveness, and a whole new way of living. He becomes the archetypal contagion of generative mimesis. (To borrow some Girard language).

> Forgiveness over against grudges, grace over stinginess, abundance over scarcity, etc.... is generative mimesis. And it's the thing I'm trying to incorporate into my life (though I'm not great at it).

 Reader Comment 3

Great writing and ideas, Jonathan! I always find atonement ideas fun to read and think about.

I would offer one more atonement theory. God decided to create, perhaps ages ago, perhaps an eternity ago. Assuming God is really, really intelligent, not to mention prescient, God would have known when deciding to create that, at least during some long periods of what would result, that many beings would be caught up in unavoidable and horrific suffering. (God would also have known that much joy would result, and hopefully that there would be long, perhaps eternal periods, in which joy and communion vastly outweighs sorrow and suffering).

So even if God never directly causes suffering to any of these beings, God's decision to create has nonetheless resulted, and will further result, in ungodly levels of suffering for many beings. God regrets this of course, and God's fierce dedication to fairness and justice means that, for God to feel right about having decided to create, not only must God share in the suffering, but God must pay for the suffering, atone for it.

Of course, God's vast intelligence, sensitivity, and perceptiveness means that God knows and shares in the suffering of every being in every moment, but God also needs to *show* us that God participates in the suffering and wants to pay for it.

So God comes among us and pays the price in our sight, and we come to know that God shares suffering with us. We are not alone, abandoned in our suffering. This is one thing God did when Jesus of Nazareth let God in all the way and shared the fullness of his life with God, holding nothing back. And this is what God does again and again throughout the vast course of cosmic history. And what God does within each of us whether we know God is there or not.

> **jonathan_foster Response**
>
> I like it . . . I especially like the "fierce dedication to fairness and justice" part. I'm banking on that! Thanks!

Reader Comment 4

I think you're wrong about downplaying the work of Christ on the cross. "There is no forgiveness without the shedding of blood."

> **jonathan_foster response**
>
> Re: "downplaying the work of Christ on the crosst . . ." If that's what it appears I'm doing, I'm not communicating well. I actually believe the work of Christ on the cross is incredibly important, particularly, as it's situated into the life of Christ within the context of his day, which was one where the religious/political/economic empire took his life. I don't downplay this at all. It means something that a brown-skinned man was executed in a state/religious sponsored act of violence.
>
> Re: forgiveness and bloodshedt . . . You're quoting Hebrews 9:22. And if you keep reading you realize it's framing this idea within and under the law. ("In fact, the law requires that nearly everything be cleansed with blood, and without the shedding of blood, there is no forgiveness.") Except, we don't live under the law and if you

flip over to chapter 10, verse 1, you'll read that "The law is only a shadow of the good things that are coming—not the realities themselves."

And then verses 4–7t . . . "It is impossible for the blood of bulls and goats to take away sins. Therefore, when Christ came into the world, he said: 'Sacrifice and offering you did not desire, but a body you prepared for me; with burnt offerings and sin offerings you were not pleased. Then I said, Here I am—it is written about me in the scroll—I have come to do your will, my God.'"

In light of love, we are being invited to have the imagination to see that Jesus didn't come to die; rather, he came to live. Sacrifice and bloodshed are more about the law (the thing we are no longer subject to) than they are about love.

However, interestingly, there is a way to see that bloodshed has always been needed. It's just that we were the ones in need of bloodshed, not God.

Propitiation is the big fancy theological word here. Someone angry or offended needs to be handled with care, pacified, or propitiated. When we humans are offended, we expect others to pay a price. And if it's true for us, then we think it must be extra true for God. If we need a pound of flesh, then God surely needs a hundred pounds of flesh. If we need propitiating, then surely, he needs super propitiating. We make sure to take this, thinking into our conceptions, definitions, and imagination about wrath and just assume the only thing that can fix this is a perfect bloody sacrifice.

But God doesn't need sacrifices. That's something we made up and projected upon God. No healthy parent needs their kid to pay in order for them to dispense love. How much more with a God of love?

 Reader Comment 5

Sacrifice is in the Bible. That's undeniable. So, how can you act as if Jesus wasn't a sacrifice? Or that sacrifice wasn't a good thing?

 jonathan_foster Response

Yes, sacrifice *is* in the bible and when we read the sacrificial passages (and the entire biblical text) through a lens of love, we might discover a story that hinges upon voluntary or involuntary sacrifice. The former leads to dialogue, flourishing, and life, while the latter leads to top-down monologue, disempowering, and death. Love might invite you to lay your life down, but love will never force you to do so. And if it does ... *it's not love.*

A Few Books and Online Resources

Atonement and Violence: A Theological Conversation, Edited by John Sanders with Hans Boersma, Hans, Scott T. Daniels, J. Denny Weaver, Thomas Finger, ©2006 by Abingdon Press

Preaching the Uncontrolling Love of God: Sermons, Essays, and Worship Elements from the Perspective of Open, Relational, and Process Theology, Jeffry Wells (Author), Nichole Torbitzky (Editor), Vikki Randall (Editor), Thomas Jay Oord (Editor), ©2024, SacraSage Press

Reading the Bible with Rene Girard: Conversations with Steven E. Berry, Michael and Lorri Hardin, ©2015, JDL Press

Saved from Sacrifice: A Theology of the Cross, S. Mark Heim, ©2006, Wm. B. Eerdmans Publishing Co

Stricken By God?: Nonviolent Identification and the Victory of Christ, Brad Jersak, Michael Hardin ©2007, William B Eerdmans Publishing Co

The Cross and the Lynching Tree James H. Cone, © 2011, Orbis Books

Atonement: A Process Perspective, Jay McDaniel (influenced by Daniel Day Williams)
https://www.openhorizons.org/atonement-a-process-perspective.html

Sin, Violence, and Forgiveness: Can Process Theology Help? Jay McDaniel
https://www.openhorizons.org/sin-violence-and-forgiveness-process-perspectives.html

Traversing Hostility: the *sine qua non* of any Christian Talk about Atonement, James Alison
https://jamesalison.com/traversing-hostility/

About the Author

Jonathan J. Foster is the partner of one, father of three, author, podcaster, co-founder and chief advocate for LoveHaiti.org. He holds a doctorate in theology from Northwind Seminary and leads OpenTable.Network, a new denominational organization empowering faith communities, pastors, chaplains, and spiritual directors in their local, missional context.

Other Books by Jonathan J. Foster

- *indigo: the color of grief*, SacraSage Press, 2024
- *Theology of Consent: Mimetic Theory in an Open and Relational Universe*, SacraSage Press, 2023

- *The Reconstructionist: Mercy>Sacrifice, People>Text, Love>Fear*, Quoir Publishing, 2022
- *Questions About Sexuality that Got Me Uninvited from My Denomination*, Verde Group, 2019

Some Other Books in the Micro Theology Series

Book 1
At-One-Ment: An Open and Relational Take on Atonement

Book 2
Love Burns like Fire: An Open and Relational Take on Hell

Book 3
Centers in the Hands of an Edgy God: An Open and Relational Take on Eschatology

Book 4
Hidden in Plain Sight: An Open and Relational Take on Sexuality

AI Disclosure

If you're looking for AI-generated writing, you're in the wrong place. My writing will always be my own work. Yes, of course, I do use software like Grammarly for copyediting—it's incredibly helpful, though, in an effort to preserve my "own voice," I find myself consistently ignoring some of its suggestions. And recently, I started using Claude.ai for some research and ideation, though what it's been most helpful for is formatting (e.g., "Claude, does the flow of my content match my Table of Contents?") So far, Claude.ai doesn't feel all that dissimilar to using a very fast, detailed, if not conversational search engine. Side note: My search engine of choice is Ecosia because, like Claude.ai's parent company, Anthropic, they seem relatively ethical. For good or for bad, friends, *everything* is relative.

ALSO FROM
SacraSage Press...

SACRASAGEPRESS.COM

Made in the USA
Coppell, TX
13 February 2026

71119958R00049